Anger Management

Unlocking Serenity - Efficacious Methods For Managing Anger To Attain Mastery Over Emotions And Anger Control

(Addressing The Root Factors Of Irritability And Anger)

Otha Humphrey

TABLE OF CONTENT

Learning About Children's Anger 1

Signs And Symptoms 36

Implementing Moments Of Respite And Unwinding Via Deep Breathing Techniques 57

What Factors Contribute To The Variation In Anger Levels Among Individuals? 66

The Developmental Phases 117

What It Symbolises And Common Qualities 133

Learning About Children's Anger

One may be inclined to assume that their child possesses an impervious nature, akin to a resilient and adaptable individual who remains unaffected by troublesome events over a prolonged period of time. Regrettably, as aforementioned, our children also experience moments of anger. Children also experience emotions with the same intensity as adults and may not possess the level of resilience that we commonly assume.

It is quite typical for your child to experience sporadic instances of meltdowns and tantrums. You may have observed occasions where they exhibit hostility or even resist authority when given a task.

I am confident that you may be interested in understanding the reasons behind your child's defiance and tantrums, as well as determining when their anger escalates into a concerning issue. When your child begins exhibiting consistent episodes of emotional outbursts, it is indeed indicative of significant distress. It is incumbent upon you to comprehend the rationale behind these recurrent displays of emotions.

There are numerous factors contributing to your child's anger and frequent defiance. It is reasonable to initially hypothesize that the cause could be an excessive allowance of freedom and a lack of emphasis on discipline in their upbringing. This could potentially be the underlying cause, although it is not universally applicable in all cases.

Your child's angry outbursts may be influenced by your own expressions of anger and lack of responsibility. It is plausible that the behavior is influenced by siblings and peers who emulate parental anger.

As you discern the underlying cause of the emotional outbursts exhibited by your child, we aim to adopt an impartial stance in order to ascertain whether their behavior stems from self-centeredness or has a valid basis. This will greatly facilitate the management of anger in children.

To comprehend and effectively handle anger, it is imperative to gain insight into the cognitive processes involved in the maturation of our offspring. The cognitive elements comprise:

Cognitive Development: The cognitive faculties of your child undergo significant growth throughout their formative years. During this timeframe, individuals acquire the knowledge of anger management techniques, which can manifest in either beneficial or detrimental ways. Now is the opportune moment for parents to collaborate closely with teachers in order to cultivate constructive approaches to managing stress.

Communication: When a child articulates their emotions, it significantly aids in their comprehension and management of said emotions. As a parent, it is important for you to comprehend that you will be required to address your children as unique individuals due to their overall proficiency in language.

Self-referential and regulatory behaviors: The self-referential behaviors encompass the tendency of your child to perceive themselves as distinct from others, functioning as a proactive and autonomous individual. Self-regulatory behaviors encompass the capacity to withstand frustration, defer immediate gratification, and exert impulse control.

What signs should I look for to ascertain if my child is exhibiting symptoms of an angry, defiant disorder?

Presented below are several indicators that ought to prompt your attention:" "Outlined here are various red flags that warrant your concern:" "Highlighted herewith are a number of signals that should give you cause for apprehension:

If your child continues to exhibit disruptive behaviors, including outbursts and tantrums, beyond the typical age range of 7-8 years when such behaviors are commonly observed.

If the manifestations of fury pose a risk to his well-being or pose a threat to those in his vicinity

If the student's frequent outbursts have escalated into a significant issue within the school environment, and the teachers have expressed concerns regarding the increasingly unmanageable nature of their behavior.

If the individual's conduct is disrupting their interactions with other children, resulting in social exclusion from their activities and gatherings.

If the individual's episodes of disruptive behavior have escalated to the point where they significantly interfere with the customary functioning of the household

If he experiences remorse following his actions stemming from his anger

The majority of parents often struggle to comprehend the underlying reasons and mechanisms behind their children's tendency to manifest intense anger that may result in harm to themselves or others. In order to tackle this issue, we will examine a few of the factors contributing to children's experience of anger.

Engage in mindful respiration - Allocate uninterrupted personal time to focus on deep breathing exercises. Attain a state of mindful awareness concerning your physical being, giving deliberate attention to a solitary, unhurried inhalation, envisioning its ascent as you subsequently exhale. Practice this procedure multiple times until you begin to experience a heightened state of relaxation.

Calming visuals - Each individual possesses their own conception of a location that induces tranquility and a sense of ease. Whether through recollection or through the creative faculties, envision a locale, individual, or possession that will assist in pacifying your state of mind. The objective of this exercise is to visualize something that elicits no emotional connection to feelings of anger or hostility.

Incorporate uplifting phrases — Remind yourself to consistently adopt a state of relaxation or tranquility. Merely engaging in mental repetition of the words on certain occasions can potentially yield the necessary diversion and certainty.

Engage in bodily relaxation – Whenever you perceive the accumulation of tension within yourself, particularly if you are accustomed to physical aggression, assume a seated position and consciously release the tension from your muscles, allowing your entire body to relax. Engaging in physical relaxation techniques can help alleviate mental distress and divert attention away from the challenging circumstances.

Healthy expression - Contrary to prevailing beliefs, engaging in aggressive forms of venting does not contribute to one's overall well-being. Punching a bag to release one's frustration is not advisable or recommended. Alternatively, should you continue to experience negative emotions regarding the altercation that transpired in the workplace, I recommend engaging in a running activity. Engaging in physical activities, including running, prompts the release of oxytocin, thus reducing stress levels within the body.

Maintaining Composure in the Midst of a Disagreement.

One of the most challenging aspects of experiencing anger is engaging in a dialogue while navigating this intricate blend of emotions. You might have developed a tendency to engage in raised voices during disputes or express statements that you do not wholly intend or anticipate remorse for, despite being unable to prevent yourself from doing so. If such is the circumstance, one can employ various tactics to ensure that a minor disagreement does not escalate into something entirely distinct.

Allow yourself some respite - In the event that you are experiencing intense aggression and anticipate that you will imminently engage in yelling during a dispute, afford yourself a period of respite. Allocate a brief period of solitude to unwind and apply the aforementioned relaxation techniques for personal rejuvenation. Over time, this behavior is expected to solidify into a habit and become a reflexive response in the face of stressful circumstances. After your condition improves, you can resume the discussion with enhanced clarity of thought.

Bear in mind the objective - Continuously reinforce within yourself that the aim of your discourse is to resolve the issue, rather than escalate it. Hence, exercise caution in ensuring that your language remains concise and direct, with the sole objective of effectively conveying your intended message, devoid of any intention to disparage, harm, or manipulate the receiver.

Maintain focus on the subject matter at hand - It is not uncommon for individuals to encounter instances where a disagreement with a partner regarding a seemingly minor matter escalates into an unrelated topic, resulting in both parties feeling drained and emotionally wounded. Ensure that you maintain focus on the specific problem under discussion, refraining from diverting attention towards unrelated issues, recollecting previous grievances and restating them, or engaging in direct personal attacks that challenge one's dignity.

●Fifth - cultivate a sense of empathy. In the event that someone has provoked your anger, it is advisable to actively engage in the mental exercise of empathizing with their perspective and endeavoring to comprehend the underlying motives behind their actions or statements. This will facilitate your recognition that their actions may not have been intended to provoke you, and will aid in your recollection that they are fellow individuals who warrant your empathy and comprehension.

●Lastly, endeavor to maintain a sense of humor and be able to find amusement in one's own actions and shortcomings. Refrain from immediate reaction and attentively consider your words during moments of anger. The likelihood is that the statements you make are rather absurd and exaggerated. It may be advisable to consider requesting your partner to document your outbursts in written form, allowing for further reflection upon them when you have regained a state of mental clarity. This exercise will facilitate your awareness of your susceptibility to overreacting, and shed light on the reasons why individuals may react to your anger by displaying disrespect or even amusement.

- Seventhly, acquire the skill of unwinding and destressing. It is essential to prioritize an adequate amount of sleep, maintain a balanced and nutritious diet, and engage in consistent physical activity. Furthermore, it would be advantageous to engage in daily meditation or yoga as part of your routine. It is imperative to exercise mindfulness towards one's own needs and subsequently take appropriate action, as this is pivotal in attaining relaxation and effectively managing anger.

One of the remarkable aspects of mindfulness meditation is its universal applicability, as it can be employed by individuals from diverse backgrounds, virtually anywhere and at any juncture. Initially, it is advisable to allocate approximately 15 minutes to secure a tranquil environment where you can settle undisturbed. After assuming a comfortable seated posture, you simply need to initiate the process by engaging in a series of deliberate and unhurried inhalations and exhalations. As you engage in this practice, strive to direct your attention towards perceiving and capturing the full extent of sensory input from each breath. Take into account the fragrances, the sensation of the air permeating your lungs, and the flavor it imparts as it glides over your tongue.

Subsequently, you ought to broaden your focus to encompass all the additional sensory input that your body is presenting. The objective of this exercise is to assist you in pacifying the incessant stream of thoughts that is likely traversing your mind. If you are able to silence those thoughts, it presents a greater opportunity to direct your attention towards the present moment and momentarily detach from your thoughts.

While you persist in your meditative state, it is probable that occasional thoughts may attempt to intrude upon your contemplation. When such an event takes place, it is imperative to refrain from actively participating in the thought or experiencing any remorse or frustration for its intrusion. Rather, it is crucial to envision the thought encapsulated within a bubble and then effortlessly allow it to drift away. Through consistent practice, you shall acquire the ability to tap into this particular frame of mind, enabling you to effectively navigate more demanding circumstances. By employing this technique, you will successfully disengage from negative thoughts during crucial discussions, allowing you to concentrate on the matter at hand.

What are the negative implications of harboring anger?

Although there exist certain instances where anger can be beneficial, such as enabling individuals to assert themselves and avoid exploitation or mistreatment, overall, anger is detrimental to our well-being. This holds particularly true when one is consistently confronted with anger and fails to adress it appropriately. There are a number of ways in which anger may have detrimental effects on both your physical well-being and overall life. These may include: 1. Experiencing negative implications on your health and well-being as a result of anger. 2. Witnessing adverse effects on various aspects of your life due to anger. 3. Encountering detrimental consequences to your health and overall lifestyle as a result of anger.

Raised blood pressure: The physiological arousal experienced during moments of anger engages the fight or flight mechanism, serving to ready the body for perceived threats or attacks. Given that you are not genuinely under attack, this situation merely elevates your blood pressure. If one experiences a persistent activation of the fight or flight response, it could potentially have an impact on cardiovascular health.

Cognitive challenges: When experiencing anger, it is probable that one may encounter difficulties with memory retention. This occurs as a consequence of the overwhelming extent to which emotion hijacks our cognitive faculties, resulting in a perceptual impediment that hinders the clarity of our recollections. This may not be excessively problematic when it comes to occasional anger, but should it occur on a frequent basis, it can certainly give rise to complications in terms of your memory.

Cardiac distress: In the event of a significant surge in blood pressure, it is probable that your heart is experiencing an increased workload as it endeavors to manage the emotional stress you are encountering.

Difficulty with interpersonal relationships: Individuals who consistently grapple with anger may encounter significant challenges in sustaining personal connections. Eventually, the accumulated frustration will manifest itself, and in the event that it escalates into aggression, the other party will swiftly be removed from the equation. You might encounter challenges in interpersonal dynamics, whether it be with a romantic partner, family members, colleagues, or individuals in various spheres of your life.

Difficulty retaining employment: In the event that you encounter challenges in maintaining personal relationships, it is plausible that you may encounter difficulties in maintaining composure when dealing with superiors and individuals occupying higher positions within the organization. This may result in difficulty maintaining the correct posture.

Headaches: Given the heightened stress resulting from persistent anger alongside the intensified blood flow due to high blood pressure, it is probable that frequent anger will lead to a significant increase in headache occurrences.

Musculoskeletal discomfort: Prolonged tension resulting from anger inevitably leads to the gradual onset of soreness and tension in the neck, back, and other muscular regions.

Insomnia: Instances may arise where you experience a difficulty in achieving restful sleep. If one harbors resentment while grappling with anger, such ruminations may cause sleep disturbance. Furthermore, if such thoughts continue to provoke an anger that persists, it is important to consider that elevated blood pressure will not contribute positively to the situation at hand.

Evidently, anger is accompanied by numerous consequential matters.

Experiencing intermittent bouts of anger may not be excessively concerning, however, a persistent state of anger can have detrimental effects on both mental and physical well-being. Discovering strategies to decrease your anger will greatly impact the level of contentment and satisfaction you experience in your life.

What progress, you inquire, have I achieved? I have initiated the process of developing a positive relationship with myself.

-Hecato

Self-compassion Increases Self-awareness

Upon initiating the practice of self-compassion, I commenced to recognize the incalculable worth it holds. I have come to perceive that self-compassion ought not to be regarded as an evasion tactic or a means to elude accountability for one's actions. Indeed, the practice of self-compassion facilitates the genuine and optimal development of one's own identity. It provides individuals with an emotional safeguard that allows for the recognition of their shortcomings and errors, without subjecting oneself to excessive self-criticism and remorse.

In order to facilitate personal development and progress, it is imperative to objectively and sincerely examine one's mistakes and failures. Nevertheless, it is imperative that you incorporate an integration of self-evaluation with utmost self-acknowledgment. Thankfully, by engaging in the practice of self-compassion, you will be able to cultivate self-love despite the ongoingendeavorto modify the aspects of your conduct that require refinement.

Dr. Carl Rogers, an esteemed figure in the field of humanistic psychology, espoused the belief that individuals require compassionate comprehension and affirmative consideration in order to undergo personal transformation. It is anticipated that you possess loved ones in your life who bestow upon you unwavering affection and esteem. Equally crucial to the presence of affectionate and benevolent individuals in one's life is the imperative of extending compassion, kindness, and patience towards oneself.

Initially, engaging in self-compassion may seem unfamiliar. Similar to acquiring any novel skill, incorporating it into your life requires dedicated practice and a considerable amount of time. Below are a handful of approaches to start integrating self-compassion into your daily regimen:

Self-compassion does not entail complacency or attempting to rationalize the justifiability of one's angry outburst. Self-compassion entails confronting one's shortcomings and errors with sincerity, without engaging in self-flagellation.

-Del Hickson

1. Treat yourself in the same manner as you would treat others.

When faced with the urge to engage in self-criticism, it is worthwhile to reflect on the advice one would extend to a peer, acquaintance, or loved one who is reproaching themselves for an error committed. It is highly probable that you would endorse and provide assistance to the individual in question. You would assist them in directing their attention towards the positive aspects, specifically the valuable lessons they have derived from the situation. If this approach has proven successful for others, it is equally suitable for you.

According to the scripture in the Bible, it is written in Matthew 22:39 that Jesus commands believers to demonstrate a profound affection towards others, treating them with the same care and consideration with which they treat themselves. It is imperative to acknowledge that Jesus does not advocate for self-neglect or subjecting oneself to harsh treatment. In contrast, Jesus conveyed that one should extend affection towards oneself. Cultivating a comprehensive, self-affirming attitude encompasses actively tending to one's physical, emotional, and spiritual well-being. This encompasses sufficient periods of rest, relaxation, and revitalization.

For many individuals, the concept of self-love may elicit a sense of unease or discomfort. One could mistakenly conflate it with exhibiting self-centeredness and self-indulgence. Nevertheless, by harboring self-affection and exhibiting benevolence towards oneself, an individual becomes more proficient in extending love and support to others.

If one fails to prioritize self-care, it is prevalent to experience a sense of exploitation or being taken for granted by others. You begin to develop the perception that individuals hold high expectations for you and demonstrate insufficient gratitude. This gives rise to a sense of aversion towards their expectations and demands, consequently precipitating further episodes of furious outbursts.

Derive wisdom from your errors and grant yourself forgiveness, thereby enhancing your state of happiness.

-Roy Bennett

Prioritize your personal oxygen mask placement before assisting others.

Upon boarding an aircraft, prior to departure, the flight attendant provides instructions regarding the fastening of seat belts, locates the emergency exits, and utters the following announcement:

In the unlikely occurrence of an abrupt decrease in cabin pressure, oxygen masks will be released. Please apply the mask to cover both your mouth and nose and proceed to breathe in a regular manner. In the event that you are accompanied by an infant or a young child during your travels, kindly ensure that you prioritize your own safety by donning your own oxygen mask before rendering assistance to others.

In the absence of sufficient levels of oxygen, the optimal functioning of our cognitive faculties is compromised. We experience a deterioration in our cognitive abilities, rendering us incapable of carrying out even the most basic of tasks. However, in the event of an aircraft emergency, what would be our initial course of action? The majority of individuals would encounter challenges in prioritizing the placement of face coverings on their children prior to attending to their own needs.

The counsel to prioritize the donning of your own oxygen mask before assisting others is not limited to emergency situations aboard an aircraft; rather, it bears relevance to all aspects of life. In the event of experiencing extreme respiratory distress and imminent loss of consciousness, one's ability to render assistance to others becomes severely compromised. Without attending to your own needs, you will be unable to provide for your family.

Failing to attend to your personal needs and subjecting oneself to harsh treatment can significantly deplete one's energy and enthusiasm. You possess limited residual energy to provide assistance, even when you have the intention to do so. Ultimately, it is impossible to extract any substance from a vessel that lacks contents.

If one's benevolence fails to encompass oneself, it remains insufficient in its entirety.

-Jack Kornfeld

2. Exercise Caution with your Language – It Holds Significance!

Individuals who encounter persistent anger often tend to develop a tendency to excessively engage in self-criticism. In the event of committing an error or succumbing to anger, individuals may resort to referring to themselves in derogatory terms such as "stupid" or "idiot." The act of labeling oneself as a jerk, a dummy, a loser, or an angry idiot may appear to be innocuous. Nevertheless, empirical investigations have demonstrated that one's verbal expressions possess substantial efficacy, exerting a profound impact on one's conduct, either yielding positive outcomes or manifesting detrimental effects upon oneself.

Self-deprecating statements not only elicit negative emotions within oneself. They exert a detrimental influence on your behavior, often operating outside your conscious awareness. On the other hand, utilizing affirmative and supportive language can enhance your determination and facilitate prudent decision-making. Although it may appear improbable, empirical research has substantiated this claim. As an illustration, a research conducted in the Netherlands exhibited how a short-term exposure to specific vocabulary had an impact on the decision-making of consumers in grocery stores and restaurants, prompting them to opt for healthier food choices.

In two distinct investigations, examiners distributed pamphlets to patrons upon their entry into a grocery establishment and a dining establishment. A subset of the promotional brochures displayed multiple terms pertaining to the reduction of body mass. Although it is unlikely that those who received these flyers were consciously cognizant of it, they were subtly prompted to recall their weight-loss objectives. They acquired more nutritious food products in contrast to customers who did not receive the specialized flyers.

It is noteworthy that a concise exposure to specific vocabulary had a discernible impact on customers' decision-making towards healthier food options. If the efficacy of a mere few written words in instilling determination within individuals is to be acknowledged, one can only fathom the tremendous outcomes that may be achieved through adopting a self-dialogue that exudes motivation and support. What can be anticipated as an outcome if you consistently endeavor to cultivate thoughts that emanate self-compassion? Not only will you experience enhanced happiness, but you will also cultivate increased motivation towards diligently undertaking your anger management program.

Exercise caution in your choice of words, whether you are engaging in internal reflection or engaging in conversation with others. This is particularly crucial in the aftermath of allowing your anger to get the best of you or engaging in hurtful behavior towards a beloved individual. One might typically find themselves thinking, "She likely has developed animosity towards me." What prompted me to raise my voice and refer to her as a self-centered individual? I fear that I may be perceived as a woeful individual, destined for a future characterized by solitariness and despair.

This form of negative self-dialogue exhibits an excessive degree of severity and inaccuracy. Moreover, it proves to be entirely ineffectual as it lacks the ability to assist in temper management. Instead, direct your attention towards the precise vocabulary you employ to depict yourself, and replace the self-deprecating words with kinder and more supportive expressions.

Signs And Symptoms

Once you have dedicated time to discerning the factors that incite your anger, it would be prudent to investigate if there exist any indicators that may be striving to capture your notice. Intense bouts of rage have the capacity to induce bodily transformations encompassing physical, emotional, and psychological aspects. Failure to address your anger may potentially jeopardize your well-being.

Several physiological indicators of anger-related issues include:

• Fatigue or lack of motivation may be experienced.

• During episodes of anger, individuals may experience a sensation of tightness in the chest accompanied by an accelerated heart rate.

• Higher blood pressure

- Episodes of dizziness or lightheadedness
- It is possible that you will encounter headaches or tension aches within the sinus cavity.
- Digestive problems
- Colds or flus
- Decreased food intake or excessive food consumption
- Diminished sexual drive • Decreased libido • Reduced sexual inclination
- Hyperventilation

Several affective manifestations may encompass:

- Depression
- Anxiety
- Self-harm
- Mood swings
- Hopelessness

Several psychological symptoms may encompass the following:

- Self-blame
- Suicidal thoughts
- Lack of concertation
- Pessimism

This compilation merely offers a condensed enumeration of the typical indicators exhibited by individuals experiencing issues with anger or rage. This compilation aims to assist you in identifying the fundamental issues you are currently facing, enabling you to discover an optimal solution tailored to your specific circumstances. If any of these symptoms are observed to significantly impact your daily functioning, I strongly advise that you seek assistance from a qualified professional. A comprehensive examination and consultation with your healthcare provider may also facilitate the process of putting yourself back on a trajectory towards optimal health.

We kindly request that you refrain from disregarding the signs and symptoms that manifest, as our bodies possess remarkable discernment. If you neglect to address these emotions, your physique will manifest an alternate issue as a means of capturing your awareness. Prioritize your well-being in order to mitigate potential health issues down the line.

IMPLEMENTING VARIOUS STRATEGIES IN MANAGEMENT

These methodologies possess the potential to alleviate individuals' stress levels or divert their attention for sufficient duration, enabling them to engage in a rational and productive contemplation process. Various strategies are effective for individuals in distinctive ways; the crucial aspect is to discover an approach that is suitable for one's specific needs and circumstances. They include:

- Engage in deliberate, unhurried respiration: Direct your attention to every breath as it enters or leaves your body, endeavor to prioritize exhalation by spending a longer duration exhaling than inhaling.

• Alleviating physical stress: Experiment with contracting and releasing each body part for a duration of 10 seconds.

• Mindfulness: The practice of meditation exemplifies one of the many techniques used to cultivate mindfulness, which can effectively redirect the mind's focus away from anger during situations that trigger such emotions. This is particularly true when the practice of mindfulness becomes a regular and dedicated habit.

• Physical exertion: Engaging in physical activity offers a highly effective means of expending the surplus adrenaline within the body. Engaging in a vigorous jog or stroll, or participating in combat-oriented disciplines like boxing or martial arts, can prove beneficial for individuals experiencing heightened aggressive emotions.

- Utilize diversionary tactics: Engaging in activities like rhythmic movement to lively music, indulging in a soothing shower, or immersing oneself in constructive tasks such as building, repairing, writing, or sketching can effectively offer respite from the matter at hand.

A few amongst us may lack the capability to accomplish these tasks individually. Therefore, it is imperative that you seek assistance from a professional. Moreover, the underlying source of the anger may necessitate seeking guidance from a professional. Factors such as legal involvement, persistent suppression of anger, frequent occurrence of intense conflicts with acquaintances, loved ones, or coworkers, engagement in physical altercations or confrontations, perpetration of domestic violence or verbal intimidation, destruction of property during episodes of anger, uncontrolled outbursts, and reckless behavior.

The emergence of anger issues is infrequent in isolation; rather, they are typically correlated with other psychological conditions, such as alcoholism, bipolar disorder, schizotypal personality disorders, psychotic disorder, and borderline personality disorder.

Attending to fundamental factors can contribute to mitigating imbalanced emotional reactions, such as anger. On certain occasions, however, individuals may find it necessary to exercise command over their anger on its own conditions.

Management therapy may be conducted in group sessions or individual consultations with a counselor or psychotherapist. In the context of anger management training, individuals acquire strategies and techniques to:

• identify triggers

• provide a constructive response, either during the initial phases of anger or in advance

- manage the stimuli

- Modify illogical and excessive cognitive patterns

- revert to a tranquil and serene condition • regain a composed and harmonious state • restore to a placid and tranquil state • come back to a state of tranquility and serenity • reinstate a state of calm and peace

- Articulate emotions and desires assertively yet calmly in circumstances known to elicit anger and frustration.

- allocate energy and resources towards resolving a problem. • channel energy and resources towards addressing a problem. • focus energy and resources on finding a solution to a problem. • dedicate energy and resources to resolving a problem. • mobilize energy and resources in order to solve a problem. • utilize energy and resources for the purpose of solving a problem.

MANAGING ANGER DURING FACE-TO-FACE ENCOUNTERS

Hostility frequently arises when engaging with others. Acquiring the skills to effectively handle this matter can mitigate the ramifications of the anger and facilitate the resolution of the root cause. There are several approaches to effectively managing our anger during confrontational situations such as:

• refraining from using terms such as "constantly" or "perpetually," which may distance individuals and hinder someone experiencing intense or illogical anger from accepting the possibility of a situation evolving.

• Release any feelings of resentment, as harboring grudges has the potential to intensify anger, thereby impeding one's ability to manage it.

• Refrain from using acerbic or scornful humor; instead, aim for amiable humor that aids in diffusing anger and fostering goodwill.

Upon coming to a halt, you are free to commence the intake of a deep breath. For the purpose of counteracting your body's reaction, it is imperative that this breath surpasses a mere inhalation and exhalation in its regular form. This respiration should originate from your diaphragm situated in the abdominal region, as opposed to your thoracic area. One can ensure proper diaphragmatic breathing by positioning their hands on their abdomen. Inhale gradually, as this facilitates the intake of a greater volume of air. It is important to take note of the expansion of your abdomen during inhalation. This breathing technique is the most elementary in nature. A more comprehensive iteration of this technique is referred to as "diaphragmatic breathing." It can be performed in a seated or supine position, provided it is conducive to your comfort. You replicated the gesture of placing your hand on your abdomen, precisely beneath the ribcage, as you had done previously. On this occasion, however, you place your alternate hand upon your chest. Commence inhaling deeply through your nasal passages, allowing your abdomen to extend and exert pressure against your hand. Your chest should not move during the process. When exhaling, gently pucker your lips and focus on perceiving the sinking motion of your hand as it moves inward with your abdomen. The procedure may be iterated a minimum of two times or a maximum of approximately nine to ten times. Ensure that each breath is given ample time, instead of rushing through them. Excessive or vigorous respiration during a breathing exercise can potentially induce the condition of hyperventilation. There is also speculation among certain individuals regarding the necessity or impact of employing nasal involvement during these exercises. There exist several advantages associated with the utilization of your olfactory organ in these exercises. An advantageous aspect is that inhalation through the nasal passage results in the humidification of the incoming air, thereby alleviating the strain on the lungs. An additional advantage is that the act of exhaling through the nostrils helps to eliminate certain bacteria and debris that may have accumulated within the nasal passages. An alternative method of nasal breathing that can be employed is referred to as alternate nostril breathing. The process can be described as follows: you begin by occluding one nostril with your thumb while inhaling deeply, then promptly switch to the other nostril and occlude it with your finger while exhaling fully.

There exist additional intricate breathing techniques; however, individuals in the early stages of anger management would benefit from commencing their practice with these more basic breathing techniques. It is also beneficial to close your eyes during the performance of your breathing exercises. It is recommended that one engage in the practice of visualizing uplifting mental imagery, such as envisioning oneself in a state of relaxation on a tranquil beach. An alternative phrasing in a more formal tone could be: "An approach to visualization involves the act of closing one's eyes and deliberately conjuring a mental image wherein the air being inhaled becomes perceptible, appearing tranquil and aesthetically pleasing. Within this mental construct, one imagines this positive air entering the lungs and subsequently permeating through the entirety of one's body." During exhalation, envision that the expelled air is visibly laden with negativity and stress as it exits your lungs, subsequently departing from your physique. Certain individuals find that providing descriptions or utilizing visual imagery aids them in mastering respiratory techniques. If this approach does not appear effective for your specific circumstances, you may consider exploring alternative strategies to identify what proves efficacious.

Alternate, more intricate methods of controlling respiration can be employed once it has been ascertained that the basic breathing technique is insufficient. Circular breathing is a prominently employed technique. This entails the act of inhaling and exhaling deeply and consistently to establish a continuous cycle of breath. Circular breathing involves a continuous flow of breath without any specific moment of breath retention, hence the term "circle". An alternative technique known as box breathing entails inhaling for a count of four, retaining breath for a count of four, exhaling for a count of four, and holding breath after exhaling for a count of four. This methodology has been determined to be effective in situations characterized by high levels of stress.

Additionally, there exists a meticulously regulated breathing technique referred to as the 4-7-8 technique. On this occasion, you will initiate the breathing exercise by inhaling through your nasal passages rather than through your oral cavity. Take a gradual breath in through your nostrils while enumerating to four. After reaching the count of four, please hold your breath until the subsequent count, but refrain from doing so until reaching the number seven. Upon reaching the number seven, commence a gradual exhalation through your oral cavity, maintaining the duration for a period of eight seconds. It is recommended that this cycle be repeated a minimum of two to three times. Additional numerical variations of breathing techniques are available, which entail the act of quantifying the number of breaths being undertaken. One method involves taking a set of twenty rapid breaths, followed by a single deep inhalation through the nostrils. It might be advisable to experiment with various counting techniques in order to determine the most effective approach for you.

It is conceivable that individuals might harness the capacity to develop their own personalized respiratory technique. In a state of relaxation, direct your attention towards the sensations in your body and the rhythm of your breath. Subsequently, you may proceed to apply the respiration technique employed during moments of tranquility whenever you sense your anger escalating beyond your control.

Regulating one's breath not only aids in managing other emotions, but it has been discovered to be highly advantageous in the realm of anger management. Engaging in the practice of deliberate and regulated breathing techniques will prove advantageous in your pursuit of anger management.

Fury can be instrumental in achieving one's desires.

How can one ascertain their specific requirements? I kindly request you to take heed of your feelings of anger. For instance, in the event that you experience physiological discomfort while journeying back to your residence subsequent to a protracted and taxing day at your occupation, and subsequently encounter a state of immobilization due to vehicular congestion. Subsequently, your companion who has experienced an exceptionally tranquil day requests your assistance in preparing dinner or procuring groceries. Therefore, it indicates that you are experiencing considerable fatigue and that your partner should commence contributing more.

The emotion of anger aids in the establishment of personal boundaries.

Do you experience a heightened sense of gastric activity whenever you encounter your parents? It is possible that they will raise queries for which you currently lack information. It is possible that inquiries could be made regarding when you anticipate securing a more promising employment opportunity, establishing a stable relationship, starting a family, or expanding your current family unit. Should you encounter any feelings of discomfort, it would be advisable to establish clear boundaries. It is appropriate to request that inquiries pertaining to my profession, romantic life, and future family plans be deferred for a certain period of time.

Anger can be instrumental in achieving goals.

Are you disheartened by the apparent lack of recognition from your supervisor towards the dedicated efforts you invest? You have the opportunity to channel your anger towards pursuing a career that offers greater fulfillment. Are you perturbed by the presence of income disparity or a disparity in wages based on gender? Utilize the emotion of anger to actively engage in activism or take tangible actions towards effecting change in the given circumstance. When channeled appropriately, anger can serve as a catalyst for achievement.

Expressing anger can potentially foster stronger bonds in relationships.

Many individuals hold the belief that anger is an undesirable emotion. It appears that they hold the viewpoint that engaging in conflicts with a partner is not preferable. I kindly request that you refrain from holding the assumption. Expressing frustration has the potential to enhance a bond in a partnership. One gains a genuine comprehension of their partner's boundaries and needs solely through the occurrence of conflicts and disagreements. Equanimity is established within a relationship solely through collaborative efforts, ensuring resolution of any disparities or disputes that may arise. By succumbing to the fear of anger or apprehension towards others' displeasure, you effectively constrain yourself from taking any action whatsoever. This implies that you have a tendency to avoid both situations and individuals that may evoke undesired emotions. Thus, does emotional discomfort possess any inherent benefits? Indeed, the affirmative response is affirmative. Nonetheless, it is imperative that you refrain from allowing your anger to dictate your actions. Harboring anger is only beneficial when one possesses the ability to manage and channel it in a constructive manner. If one is unable to effectively regulate their anger, it will only result in personal discontentment.

Myths About Anger

Anger is widely regarded as one of the most potent emotions that an individual can encounter. Nevertheless, it is frequently misconstrued. Regrettably, the entirety of anger-related misconceptions often lead to maladaptive conduct. The subsequent content will elucidate the fallacies and verities surrounding the emotion of anger.

Anger is consistently associated with negative outcomes.

Kindly acknowledge that experiencing anger is acceptable and permissible. Rage is not solely an ordinary sentiment, but rather it is considered to be highly beneficial for one's well-being. As previously stated, anger can be advantageous when channeled appropriately. History demonstrates that judiciously harnessing anger can prove advantageous. Numerous instances of social injustices were rectified through the catalyst of societal discontent. What would have transpired in the annals of history if Martin Luther King, Jr. had never harbored any resentment?

Implementing Moments Of Respite And Unwinding Via Deep Breathing Techniques

Timeouts

The implementation of a timeout is a straightforward yet effective tactic for managing anger, which merits inclusion in the anger management strategies of all individuals. You have the option to utilize timeout in a formal or informal manner. In its fundamental essence, timeout can be defined as the act of engaging in a deliberate practice of deep breathing and contemplation prior to responding, rather than impulsively reacting. It could also entail ceasing the dialogue that is inciting your anger or departing from the circumstance that is precipitating the intensification. The formal application of timeout pertains to interpersonal connections, encompassing companionship, familial ties, and professional interactions. A period of reflection and solitude serves as a crucial mechanism for managing anger, as it can be adeptly employed amidst heightened emotions. Allow me to provide you with instructions on how to initiate a timeout.

Exercise patience by taking a moment to reflect before engaging in communication or taking any action.

To facilitate relaxation, lower your shoulders and engage in deep breathing. You are experiencing anger, which prompts your instincts to prepare your body for combat. However, through the implementation of a timeout, your rational self can intervene and counteract this physiological response by instructing your body to become calm.

In the event that you experience an inclination to strike or hurl an object, it is advised to either cease the conversation or withdraw from the situation, followed by directing your anger towards an object such as a cushion that is devoid of harmful potential to both yourself and others.

If you believe it might be beneficial, feel free to vocalize loudly. In the presence of others, you may choose to assuage your tension by vocalizing into a cushion or pillow.

Engage in self-reflection to attain a sense of tranquility. Envision the actions or words that would be demonstrated by an individual renowned for their composure, and adopt their approach or counsel oneself accordingly.

Imagine yourself in a state of calm and ease.

Extract yourself from the tense situation or divert your attention elsewhere. Engage in solving a crossword puzzle, peruse a magazine, take a leisurely stroll, or indulge in the pleasure of listening to calming music.

Strategies for ensuring the successful implementation of your timeout

Plan beforehand for timeouts. They ought not to exhibit abrupt or unforeseeable characteristics. Preemptively consider potential activities or destinations to engage in during a period of respite.

Practice continuously. With increased practice, the time-outs will become more manageable for you.

Please be advised that timeouts do not constitute acts of fleeing or escaping. Consistently endeavor to address the situation with composure and efficiency.

Beforehand, it is advisable to notify individuals of your intention to take breaks, with the purpose of preventing escalating moments of irritation and anger. Your commitment will be appreciated by the rest of the group.

Despite their efficacy as a means of anger management, timeouts may not be universally applicable in all scenarios. Consequently, it would be advisable to employ alternative approaches and strategies in order to effectively manage and mitigate your anger.

Relaxation Through Breathing

Engage in a deep-breathing exercise as a means to alleviate feelings of tension, irritation, and anger whenever they arise. Through the utilization of this technique, one directs their attention towards their breath and endeavors to alleviate any bodily tension that may be present. Here are the directions:

Please assume a comfortable seated position and, if desired, gently close your eyes or fix your gaze downwards.

Please allow yourself a brief moment to compose and center yourself. Develop an awareness of your bodily sensations and conduct a thorough examination for any signs of tension, commencing from the soles of your feet and gradually progressing towards the top of your head. Please be mindful of any potential tension that may be present in your feet, ankles, legs, abdomen, arms, hands, shoulders, neck, and facial muscles. Endeavor to release any form of tension.

Develop mindfulness of your respiration as it enters and exits your physical being. The act of respiration can bestow a profound sense of relaxation. Inhale deeply, with a calm and measured breath, and observe the rise and fall of your chest as your lungs expand. Exhale gradually through the nostrils. Once more, inhale softly and deeply, allowing your chest and lungs to be filled with air. Pause briefly and observe the quantity of air you are capable of inhaling. Subsequently exhale by slowly releasing your breath. Once more, inhale gradually and completely. Please retain the breath momentarily before exhaling.

For a brief duration, maintain this breathing technique while directing your attention exclusively towards your breath. With every inhalation and exhalation, you will experience a gradual deepening of relaxation within your body. Alleviate any lingering tension through controlled respiration.

Once more, inhale deeply and fully draw in your breath. Retain the breath momentarily and subsequently exhale. Inhale once more, retain your breath momentarily, and subsequently exhale. Maintain your concentration on your respiration as it enters your thoracic cavity and permeates your pulmonary organs. Once more, inhale deeply, retain your breath momentarily, and then exhale.

Please activate your visual perception when you sense that you are prepared. How was the exercise? How are you currently experiencing your emotions? Have you experienced any novel sensations during the process of respiration?

You lead a rather hectic lifestyle, and thus, this particular breathing exercise can be condensed to a mere 3-4 cycles of inhaling and exhaling deeply. Please bear in mind that engaging in this brief exercise has the potential to effectively aid in your relaxation when you find your anger intensifying. Engage in the physical activity while in motion, during your commute, at your place of employment, during periods of anticipation, or even within the confines of your dwelling. Engage in regular repetitions of this deep-breathing technique and employ it across diverse circumstances.

What Factors Contribute To The Variation In Anger Levels Among Individuals?

Moreover, there exist various individual factors that exert an impact on our inclination towards experiencing anger.

Aggressive Personalities

Certain individuals have been endowed with particularly assertive dispositions. Despite the potentially negative connotations of the word "aggressive," there are practical applications for individuals possessing this particular personality trait. These individuals display a strong inclination towards competitiveness. They demonstrate a willingness to confront and embrace challenges.

Frequently, they exhibit a positive and proactive mindset. They exhibit a preference for taking action as opposed to adopting a passive "wait and see" approach. Due to their inherent propensity for competition, they exhibit unwavering determination in the pursuit of their objectives.

However, the aggressive personality does come with its share of drawbacks. Due to their unrelenting pursuit of victory, their leadership can be characterized by high expectations and demanding standards. Their vitality and liveliness may prove overwhelming for individuals who have a preference for a more subdued and less vigorous approach to existence.

In circumstances where there is a lack of substantial development, individuals exhibiting assertive qualities may also demonstrate a sense of impatience. When they assume leadership, they also display a propensity for exerting dominance over others and fearlessly confronting those who oppose them.

Individuals exhibiting such a disposition invariably encounter conflict when interacting with others. They are inclined to find themselves in circumstances where anger can be deemed justifiable. Due to their strong desire for success, they might encounter increased difficulty in relinquishing arguments.

If one possesses such a personality trait, it is imperative to modulate one's assertiveness in alignment with the specific objective at hand and the diverse individuals one engages with. At times, it becomes imperative to prioritize interpersonal connections above objectives and accomplishments.

Substance Abuse

Additionally, individuals may succumb to a lack of emotional and behavioral restraint as a result of substance misuse. Certain substances, such as alcohol and certain drugs, have a tendency to compromise an individual's cognitive faculties, leading to inhibited decision-making abilities. Individuals under the influence of drugs and alcohol fail to exercise sufficient cognitive deliberation. They express their thoughts openly.

When provoked, individuals intoxicated by substances tend to lose their inhibitions. Ordinary individuals would endeavor to mitigate the escalation of their anger in view of the potential enduring consequences. Inebriated and substance-affected individuals demonstrate limited consideration for prospective outcomes. They have a tendency to prioritize the present moment. Should they become enraged, they will unapologetically articulate their anger.

Alternative formulation in a formal tone: "Alternative substances display more subdued effects, yet can still contribute to exacerbating feelings of anger." For example, caffeine has been observed to elevate heart rates, enhance alertness, and modulate our emotional states. If one is predisposed to experiencing anger, the excessive consumption of the substance will heighten the probability that even the slightest provocation will elicit anger.

Blaming other people

Certain individuals experience frustration due to their tendency to attribute blame. In instances where events do not transpire according to their desires, they seek out individuals to hold accountable for such outcomes. Rather than proceeding to the next course of action, they have a tendency to direct their focus towards assigning blame to individuals.

Individuals inclined towards assigning blame are also more predisposed to experience eventual failure in life. They excessively prioritize assigning blame for their misfortune instead of proactively considering strategies to overcome it. Individuals who excessively attribute responsibility are consistently filled with anger towards the individual they perceive as accountable. In order to assume control over one's anger, it is imperative to abstain from developing a pattern of attributing blame to others. To accomplish this objective, here are several measures that can be undertaken:

Direct your attention towards the process of recuperation and restoration.

Individuals who tend to engage in the act of attributing blame are exemplified by those who have experienced victimization through criminal offenses or have sustained work-related injuries. Individuals who excessively assign culpability to the wrongdoers are less likely to emerge from the experience unharmed.

Individuals who assign responsibility for their injuries to their employers exhibit decreased likelihood of being reintegrated into the workforce. If they were to be rehired, they exhibit a significant amount of counterproductive work conduct which could potentially lead to their demotion or termination.

Individuals who fail to grant absolution for the offenses they have endured are at a higher risk of experiencing post-traumatic stress disorders.

In such instances, it is advisable to extend forgiveness to the individuals accountable for the adversities we have encountered, redirecting our efforts and concentration towards recovery and the restoration of our lives.

5

Manifestations of Anger

There exist various forms of anger. Various factors elicit anger within us, each for unique rationales. By acknowledging the specific category of anger you are encountering, you will be empowered to manage it effectively. Prior to exploring various strategies for anger management, we shall endeavor to ascertain the precise nature of your anger.

Manifestation of Anger: Individuals exhibiting behavioral anger tend to directly confront the stimuli that provoke their anger. Typically, it is individuals other than oneself. This confrontation usually commences with verbal discourtesy and frequently progresses into physical aggression.

Individuals who suffer from chronic anger are those who harbor strong animosity towards the world and its inhabitants, including themselves, often unable to articulate the underlying reasons for such intense hostility. They tend to become overtly agitated at the slightest provocation, exhibiting frequent fits of anger.

Constructive Anger: Frequently arising from the application of anger management methods, individuals harness their anger in a constructive manner to attain their desired outcomes.

Intentional Anger: Your employer could serve as a compelling illustration of intentional anger. It is frequently utilized as a strategy to exert authority over subordinates and typically has a limited duration.

The emotion of critical anger often arises from individuals with diminished self-worth, who tend to manifest their anger by publicly denigrating others as a means to enhance their own perceived superiority.

Intense Rage: Precisely as stated. These individuals are so consumed by their anger that they are unable to endure it any longer. They frequently resort to acts of devastation or hostility, including physical aggression, leading to injury or harm to both themselves and others.

Unjustifiable Fury: This form of anger is entirely lacking in justifications. Typically, as a result of diminished self-worth, individuals perceive hostility from others and consequently react with anger and aggression as a means of retaliating against their perceived antagonist.

Repressed Agitation: Individuals who exhibit passive anger predominantly resort to sarcasm or mockery as a means to channel their anger, and actively avoid engaging in direct confrontations or conflicts. This typically evokes further frustration within themselves due to their inability to directly manage the source of their anger.

Indignant Fury: Perhaps the most prevalent form of anger, this arises as a direct reaction in response to another individual's outburst or actions that provoke anger within oneself.

Self-imposed anger is a variety of anger that individuals employ as a means of self-retribution for perceived wrongdoing. They may engage in self-inflicted injuries, excessive consumption of food, or even resort to self-imposed starvation.

Verbal Anger: Anger expressed verbally rather than through physical means. Individuals who encounter verbal frustration employ derogatory language and disparaging remarks in order to belittle and inflict psychological harm upon others.

Explosive anger: When an emotion is described as volatile, it indicates an explosive nature. Anger exhibits a similar pattern. This form of anger has the capacity to manifest suddenly and exhibit severe levels of aggression. It frequently appears and disappears without any prior notice.

These are the predominant forms of anger. Do you perceive any of those attributes within your own self? As previously mentioned, varying forms of anger manifest in diverse circumstances. And that which provoked annoyance within you yesterday may not even affect you today.

It is crucial to comprehend the various manifestations of anger that one may encounter, in order to effectively determine the appropriate course of action for each unique circumstance.

A Happy Song

While this perspective may not strictly adhere to professional norms, it has proven to be effective in enhancing my interactions with others. I can confidently affirm its efficacy based on personal experience, as it is a deliberate strategy that I employ to foster a more positive connection with individuals. Anger has never been a factor of concern for me. The display of impatience is nearly tantamount to an equally undesirable behavior. I developed a mechanism wherein, instead of fixating on the lethargic nature of life, I chose to mentally harmonize a joyful tune that uplifted my spirit, even amidst the presence of individuals exhibiting incompetence. That elicited a considerably more favorable response from me. It is effective for addressing anger issues as I have witnessed its successful implementation during workshops with individuals experiencing symptoms of anger. The more preposterous the composition, the more effectively it operates. Consider selecting a melodious composition of contentment to retreat to during bouts of anger, affording yourself the opportunity to cultivate a constructive reaction rather than succumbing to anger.

It is imperative that you acquire the skillset of effectively engaging with individuals, as this will enable you to foster a more expansive mindset when engaging with individuals from various walks of life. Make an effort to attend familial gatherings. Make an effort to engage in a social setting where you have the opportunity to interact with others, even if this entails enrolling in a formal educational course. You should strive to enhance your interpersonal skills, ensuring that the encounters you have with others are predominantly characterized by positive outcomes.

Hence, endeavor to associate with individuals who possess a comparable mindset. It could be beneficial for you to consider enrolling in yoga classes. Yoga imparts the knowledge of correct breathing techniques and the utilization of breath as a means to augment the body's core strength. I offer this assertion based on the fact that yoga facilitates a reduction in pace and promotes relaxation. Furthermore, it fosters connection with individuals possessing a serene demeanor, who can guide and support the cultivation of tranquility within oneself. They will assist you in acquiring valuable experience, bringing forth an entirely novel set of circumstances that effectively distances you from any prevailing sense of hostility to which you may have grown accustomed.

Should you harbor the belief that such a notion is applicable solely to a specific demographic, you are mistaken. Individuals of diverse age groups and genders derive substantial benefits from engaging in yoga, perceiving that the application of discipline during this practice enables them to exercise self-control in various real-life scenarios, including the regulation of their own anger.

4. Engaging in conflicts with other individuals who are filled with anger is not advisable, as it is unlikely that you will be able to alter their behavior or mindset. [Horace]

It is futile to attempt to alter the mindset of individuals who believe they are entitled to inflicting misery upon your existence. In order to prevent the perpetuation of this pattern of anger, it is advisable to refrain from acknowledging undesirable behavior and allow the individuals involved to engage in disputes with others until they resolve their dissatisfaction.

5. When individuals are subjected to mistreatment and denied the appropriate treatment they deserve, it is

imperative to refrain from pledging or ridiculing them. [Plato]

You may be lacking comprehension in this matter, as your efforts to persuade the individual who is angered appear to be misguided. You are likely to achieve greater success by allowing him the opportunity to express his frustrations and extending forgiveness towards him for his actions, as it is plausible that his hostility towards others stems from a history of enduring injustice throughout his lifetime.

6. In the event that anger arises, it is advisable to attempt to empathize with the other party's viewpoint, contemplating potential circumstances that may have precipitated their emotional response. [Seneca]

While it may present a challenge, it is imperative to make a conscientious effort to comprehend the perspective of individuals who exhibit anger when engaging with them. It is essential to comprehend his emotions and rationales, as verbal communication alone is insufficient to alter their perspectives.

7. Always reiterate your innocence and refrain from erroneously assessing individuals, regardless of the intensity of their anger towards you. [Plato]

It is imperative not to allow others to induce feelings of guilt within oneself based on the impact of one's actions, irrespective of their ensuing response. One should refrain from attributing blame to oneself for their anger, instead, it is advisable to discern the underlying cause. In this manner, you will effectively manage individuals expressing anger by approaching them with rationality, while refraining from anticipating their reasonableness.

8. Ensure that due consideration is given to both perspectives before undertaking any actions that may detrimentally affect either party. [Epicurus]

When your actions inflict harm upon the lives of others, it is imperative to take into account the perspectives of both parties involved. Individuals are typically accountable for a portion of their misfortunes, and it is improper to attribute personal errors or mishaps solely to external factors or others.

9. Avoid causing individuals to experience negative emotions by unnecessarily attributing their anger towards you, solely because another person has wronged them. [Aristotle]

You should resist succumbing to the pressure of others who attempt to impose feelings of guilt upon you for actions you did not commit towards them. When faced with someone's intense anger, it is imperative to attentively listen to their grievances and earnestly endeavor to manage their rage in a rational manner. Always maintain composure in their presence and refrain from criticizing them, as doing so may further fuel their anger.

\# 10. Do not retaliate against individuals who have caused harm or harbored animosity towards you. [Seneca]

Retaliation is perpetually undesirable; nonetheless, it is unrealistic to anticipate a modification in others' conduct merely based on personal desires. If someone has exhibited misconduct or affronted you, it is advisable to relinquish and disremember the incident.

\# 11. Please endeavor to grasp the concept that the world operates independently of your personal sphere, and the resolutions made by individuals will have no bearing on the trajectory of your own life. [Epicurus]

Two: Embracing Release

One of the utmost significant facets of anger management entails the dissipation of energies, or the capacity to cease clinging. I was once acquainted with an individual who derived satisfaction from a distinct sense of mastery over his surroundings. He exhibited an unwavering commitment towards maintaining the utmost cleanliness of his household, and exerted great efforts in asserting authority over nearly every aspect of his existence. His demeanor towards life rendered him a highly wrathful individual, susceptible to fits of fury. Upon encountering situations where things did not unfold according to his expectations, he frequently experienced sentiments of betrayal and harbored feelings of resentment. On one occasion, he proceeded to forcefully shatter a vase subsequent to his wife's inability to remove a few fingerprints from its base. He harbored a strong distaste towards his inability to exert full control over all aspects of his household.

Regrettably, this is the capricious essence of existence. Occasionally, the nefarious individuals emerge victorious. On occasion, individuals do not attain what is rightfully theirs. Occasionally, life exhibits an inherent lack of fairness.

By reconciling with the reality that the universe is not consistently fair, you will gain an advantage in developing skills to regulate your emotions. Frequent occurrences of anger stem from a perception of wrongdoing. It may be advantageous to recognize that within a world characterized by profound unpredictability, the assurance of justice is not invariably a given. While it is not implied that one should display apathy towards injustice, alternatively, by directing one's endeavors towards adept and strategic measures, the likelihood of personal distress could potentially be mitigated, consequentially leading to reduced suffering among the individuals in one's vicinity.

A crucial aspect of anger reduction entails relinquishing any emotional impediments that could hinder the process of healing. It could be advantageous to conceptualize your emotional being as a vacant receptacle. Every individual emotion contributes a specific quantity of fluid to the receptacle. Incompetent rage occupies a valuable allocation of your energy that could be more productively employed to enrich your existence. It is crucial to engage in the necessary introspection to carefully pour out a portion of the liquid from one's glass when it appears to be full, and to ensure that the resulting mixture of emotions is both nourishing and well-balanced. An empty glass, brimming solely with bitterness and animosity, shall leave one engulfed in solitude and consumed by fury. A vessel brimming solely with affection could render one inexperienced and incapable of safeguarding oneself within a capricious realm. Every emotion resides within the confines of your being. Every individual is indispensable, however, just as a diverse assortment of ingredients in a nutritious salad ensures optimal nourishment, variety is paramount.

Is anger capable of exerting control over one's life?

The extent to which anger is manifested will serve as the criterion by which the level of control it exerts in your life is gauged. Anger can be classified as episodic when it occurs with a frequency of approximately three to five instances per week or when it occurs infrequently. The condition can be classified as chronic if an individual experiences anger exceeding two instances or surpassing a frequency of ten occurrences within a single day. It is reasonable to assert that chronic anger necessitates anger management, whereas occasional or intermittent displays of anger are not typically regarded as problematic.

Presented herein are various classifications of instances of anger that can provide you with insight into identifying your own position within them:

Intermittent irritation

There exists a subset of individuals who experience infrequent occurrences of irritation or mild anger. The typical attributes exhibited by these individuals include being excellent companions, having a positive disposition, being laid-back, and exuding cheerfulness. There shall be no complications or issues encountered should you belong to this particular category.

Intermittent anger
The subset of individuals under observation amounting to approximately 36 percent is characterized by recurrent episodes of anger occurring on multiple occasions each week. These individuals have a tendency to experience occasional anger but display a persistent lack of proactive action in response to their emotions. The transient nature of their anger contributes to their swift ability to move on and subsequently forget.

Intermittent rage

This is an explicit manifestation of toxic anger. This occurrence is not a commonplace event, and individuals of this nature prove to be pleasant companions, provided that their ire remains dormant. Nevertheless, provoking them would be an egregious error!

Persistent irritation
Certain individuals perceive this conduct as concerning, yet it is not of grave severity. Individuals of this nature predominantly exhibit tendencies towards resentment or moodiness, yet they are generally able to tolerate one's presence on a consistent basis. A limited number of individuals belong to this category, which is highly commendable.

Persistent anger
This entails a significantly profound examination of the detrimental impact of an enraged emotion. These individuals consistently display anger over trivial matters and might hold the incorrect belief that everything is fine as long as

they do not lose control. Nevertheless, the consistent experience of anger is detrimental to one's well-being.

Persistent rage
The intense fury that individuals experience within this classification unleashes without restraint and possesses significant peril. The perceived resentment yields no advantageous outcome, thus contaminating all aspects of their existence.

The label "anger management" should be avoided when referring to individuals experiencing chronic anger issues. Rage significantly differs from anger. Anger can still be managed, however, rage has the potential to exert dominance over one's character and overall existence. Reacting with anger in response to provocation can be viewed as a constructive measure, as opposed to succumbing to a state of fury over trivial matters.

Value 1 – The Preservative value: the fundamental purpose of emotion is to protect us from an imminent danger or harm. Anger, as an inherent emotional response, is grounded in our instinctive drive to safeguard both ourselves and others from perceived threats. Anger engenders heightened vigilance and concentration, enabling us to effectively confront any peril that may arise. When provoked by someone or a particular incident, an innate anger is aroused within us, impelling us to respond defensively and shield ourselves against any form of harm or assault. This constitutes the central rationale for the positivity of anger. Humans possess an inherent aversion to pain and discomfort; consequently, anger can serve as a viable recourse when confronted with the imperative to surmount adversity.

Value 2 – The Incentive Value: what remains largely unnoticed is the driving force encapsulated in anger. When circumstances deviate from the expected trajectory, anger arises as a corrective response to rectify this phenomenon. When your child returns home at the conclusion of the academic session with subpar grades, responding with constructive anger will serve to encourage and inspire them to strive for improvement. One may refrain from uttering, "I do not desire him to experience negative emotions, and thus I choose to adopt a stance of a caring paternal figure by accepting the situation and anticipating his improvement." In instances where our endeavors do not transpire as anticipated, resentment can serve as a potent catalyst, compelling us to rectify our imperfections and excel. It serves as a means to surmount the challenges we face.

Value 3 – Goal-Oriented Value: By harnessing your anger effectively, you can attain your desired outcome. There exist objectives and aspirations that we intend to achieve. In order to achieve our objectives, the deliberate stimulation of anger would prove instrumental in attaining the desired outcome. Anger propels us towards the attainment of our objectives, obliterating any potential barriers that might impede our progress. Occasionally, one may experience a sense of dissatisfaction stemming from not yet having accomplished a predetermined objective; quite often, this sentiment serves as impetus to step out of one's comfort zone and propel oneself towards the attainment of said goal. That emotion corresponds to a manifestation of workplace frustration.

Value 4 – The Positive Outlook Value: in the face of challenges, fear, offense, and frustration, anger could serve as a fitting response to rely on. Anger instills within us a particular sense of hopeful anticipation. It enables us to transcend the suffering and unveils the magnificent aspirations we aspire to accomplish. Anger is accompanied by a sense of empowerment, instilling in us a favorable perception of our capabilities and self-worth. We have the potential to transcend our limitations and attain any goal we desire. Anger frequently functions as an indicator of social and personal values. It governs our self-perception; whenever our circumstances cause us to deviate from our values, anger undermines our moral principles and convictions.

Value 5 – The Negotiating Value: one advantage of anger is that it provides us with insights regarding our intrinsic value. In the face of others belittling us, we channel our anger into action to vocalize our dissent and vehemently oppose such behavior. Anger functions as a mechanism that enables us to safeguard our intrinsic worth whenever our value is under threat. In leveraging our emotions, engaging in negotiations could potentially yield favorable outcomes. The strategic utilization of anger for the purpose of negotiation can effectively result in the attainment of one's desired outcomes from an individual or a given circumstance. Frequently, anger in the context of negotiation tends to foster success at the bargaining table, as individuals engaged in negotiations are more likely to yield significant concessions when confronted by an individual displaying anger while making minimal demands.

7 - Exercise Restraint and Maintain Composure

You are not required to inform me of what actions ought to be taken.

On how many occasions have you uttered this statement, only to encounter severe negative consequences? How frequently have you exhibited such behavior within the previous week or month..?

Please pause for a moment and carefully consider the matter at hand. Is it not a prevalent statement that often emerges in a moment of heightened anger? The root of the matter could stem from the conduct or remarks of the individual in question, or it may be entirely disconnected from their actions. Subsequently, subsequent to this assertion...

Argument. More anger. More irritation.

There may have been instances in which individuals from your professional or personal network, such as colleagues, friends, superiors, or acquaintances, might have experienced agitation or annoyance due to your commentary or perspective. When subjected to another individual's rage, how do you respond without excessively exaggerating your own reaction? What is your rationale for considering it to be an excessive response? The primary factor behind this is your recognition that the other individual may not have fully or accurately comprehended your point, or that their response is solely influenced by their instincts, beliefs, or past experiences, which could potentially skew their judgment.

The same principle that we employ to others is likewise applicable to ourselves. It is imperative that we also extend the opportunity for others to fully elucidate their perspectives, without our interference based on past experiences and beliefs.

If you possess a comprehensive comprehension of this matter, it is plausible that you, too, would refrain from responding to their excessive emotional response. Maintain composure, exercise patience until they have concluded their remarks, and once another opportunity arises, endeavor to elucidate your perspective once more. If you do not comprehend, then undoubtedly you will exhibit an alternate response which might be:

You consistently fail to comprehend the message I am endeavoring to convey.

You consistently express dissent towards my views, even when they are intended to lead to improvement.

Given the aforementioned circumstances, what do you anticipate would be the eventual outcome? Debates would ensue, often punctuated by intense verbal exchanges. So, what is the final outcome? Again as mentioned above.Argument. More anger. More irritation.

Your companion engages in a jest at your expense. With which emotion do you correlate that specific moment? Anger.Frustration.

One effective strategy is to actively refrain from responding excessively to another individual's perspectives or remarks. This will prove advantageous not solely in scenarios where your voice goes unheard, but also when you refrain from immediate concurrence with the perspectives of others. This will be beneficial in multiple regards.

guaranteeing the presence of comprehensive and accurate communication by the conclusion

Exercise caution in order to preserve interpersonal relationships, particularly when discussing highly personal matters.

Comprehending the perspective of the other individual.

enhances your or the other person's accessibility for subsequent discussions

No matter how extensively I expound upon the advantages inherent in refraining from overreacting, the collective quantity of such advantages far surpasses any opposing arguments. Each instance in which you elect not to overreact demonstrates your mental fortitude and resilience. This fosters a positive perception of you among others, as they perceive you as someone who is receptive to their ideas and supportive in their growth rather than critical.

Exercising restraint in one's response is advantageous not only for oneself, but also for those in proximity. Throughout the course of your life, one will encounter individuals on their personal journey who consistently seek self-improvement, continuously aspiring to surpass their past accomplishments. Individuals of this nature will exert themselves to consistently remain in close proximity to you in order to acquire additional knowledge. This bears significant relevance to the field of human psychology. What is the rationale behind our inclination to peruse biographies chronicling the lives of notable individuals? Is the solution to this matter not overwhelmingly straightforward? We endeavor to emulate their lives, which have proven successful, as we hold the belief that a blueprint that has guided accomplished individuals in the past can be adapted to ensure your own personal success.

In conclusion, opting not to respond or restricting your responses will facilitate constructive dialogues and facilitate rational deliberations.

Four: The Effective Management of Anger

It is imperative for individuals afflicted with anger to acquire skills in anger management. In line with the aforementioned term, anger management entails acquiring the skills necessary to effectively regulate and address one's anger in a manner that safeguards against adverse impacts on both personal well-being and interpersonal relationships. It pertains to acquiring the skills to effectively regulate your emotions so as not to inflict harm upon yourself or those in your vicinity. The process of anger management may appear challenging, but it is in fact fairly straightforward, necessitating only steadfastness and commitment. In order to effectively manage your anger, it is imperative to possess a resolute determination to acquire the necessary skills for its control and demonstrate unwavering dedication towards mastering this capability.

In order to acquire the skill of managing anger, it is imperative to initially acknowledge and accept its detrimental impact. Certain individuals fail to acknowledge the significance of anger as a problem that necessitates resolution, thus neglecting to seek out ways to effectively manage it. Furthermore, they hold the belief that they are not the ones responsible for the problem. In contrast, their primary objective is to assign responsibility to others for their individual predicaments. Therefore, it is imperative to acknowledge and discern it as an issue that necessitates resolution. The initial step towards acquiring the ability to regulate and govern our emotions is the cultivation of self-awareness.

Upon acknowledging the issue at hand, the subsequent course of action entails identifying the underlying cause. So, I implore you to introspect and pose the ensuing inquiries to yourself:

What is the root cause of my anger?

What is the underlying cause of my anger?

What alternative strategies can I employ when experiencing anger?

In what manner has it impacted my interpersonal connections?

Do I harbor positive sentiments towards this response?

Why am I being governed by this potent sentiment?

Why am I unable to employ reason in place of allowing my emotions to dominate?

Engaging in introspection and posing such inquiries is a crucial facilitator in discerning the underlying trigger of one's anger.

Upon identifying the underlying causes or sentiments leading to the outward display of anger, the subsequent course of action entails mastering the ability to overcome this emotional state or rationale. Successfully accomplishing this task necessitates focused mental effort and unwavering determination. Once you acquire the ability to dominate the emotional aspect of your anger and maintain a firm grasp on it, you have successfully acquired the skill to oversee and regulate your anger. Exercising resilience entails acquiring the ability to effectively manage a situation that is prone to evoke anger, thus averting the manifestation of anger. It is imperative that you acquire the ability to confront and manage our fears and insecurities. It is imperative to cultivate the ability to eliminate any negative emotions that you believe serve as catalysts for your anger. It is advantageous to learn how to overcome circumstances that cause distress rather than harboring anger and resentment towards them; this understanding is essential. Outlined below are several pragmatic approaches through which you can acquire the skills to effectively control and manage your anger.

Accelerated Heartbeat

Similar to any physical activity, the human body will commence an accelerated circulation of blood, facilitated by an increase in adrenaline levels and the release of supplementary hormones that coincide with an episode of anger. Consequently, this leads to an increase in heart rate and irregularity similar to the response elicited by a sudden stimulus. On occasion, individuals may experience sensations where their heart palpitations become so intense that they perceive the sensation of it being on the verge of bursting from their chest, or they entertain thoughts that those in proximity might actually discern its beats. Frequently, it is accompanied by a sensation of tinnitus or a perception akin to being inverted, where blood appears to gather in the head.

Visibly reddened and experiencing an intense sensation of heat on the face

When the human body undergoes the fight or flight response, there is a dilation of blood vessels to facilitate the heightened blood circulation. The proximity of blood vessels to the skin's surface results in a sensation of warmth and flushing in the cheeks. This reaction resembles the physiological response exhibited when an individual experiences blushing or embarrassment, characterized by heightened warmth and flushing.

Variations of the phrase "Mild to Extreme Headaches" in a formal tone: 1. Headaches ranging from mild to severe 2. Headaches ranging in intensity from mild to extreme 3.Headaches spanning a spectrum of mildness to severity 4.Headaches exhibiting a gradient from mild to intense 5.Headaches of varying degrees, from mild to extreme.

The experience of anger leads to muscular tension, particularly manifesting in the back, neck, and even the scalp. This phenomenon induces a sensation akin to heightened pressure constricting the head, leading to the onset of a tension headache of varying intensity, ranging from mild to severe.

Excessive Perspiration

The experience of anger can lead to an elevated level of perspiration, exceeding the ordinary or even manifesting in a marked excess, as the body reacts to hormonal changes in a manner akin to engaging in strenuous physical activity or weightlifting.

Experiencing Immobilization Due to Anger

A disadvantage of anger is that individuals often become entangled in its grasp. Consequently, they fail to give heed to the fundamental inquiries: Is my current approach yielding desired results? Is it effective? Is my desired outcome being fulfilled? Reflect upon how you would respond to the inquiries pertaining to the subsequent life circumstances:

• Matrimonial relations: The repercussions of raising my voice towards my spouse Does she feel better? Do I feel better? Do we grow closer?

What actions can I undertake to effectively address the issues at hand?

• Workplace Dynamics: Exploring the repercussions of engaging in conflicts with colleagues. Is my performance viewed as impactful in the workplace? Does our work improve? What actions could I undertake to effectively address and amicably resolve our conflicts, thereby fostering a more harmonious and efficient work environment?

• Motor vehicle operation: What are the consequences of engaging in offensive verbal gestures towards fellow motorists and closely following them on the road? Do individuals demonstrate an improvement in their driving skills?

• Parenting: Consequences of vocally expressing refusal when my children persistently request something. Do they feel better? Do I feel better? Do we grow closer? What strategies can I employ to facilitate their attainment of their objectives while prioritizing their safety and mitigating any potential discomfort on my part?

Approaches to Social Problem-solving

If you adhere to the patterns of behavior exhibited by a majority of individuals, it is likely that you have established a methodical method for confronting challenges. Over time, this approach has developed into a recurrent behavioral tendency that constitutes an integral aspect of your character. According to psychological research, the majority of individuals exhibit one of three approaches in solving social problems, of which two are considered unfavorable while one is regarded as favorable.

A spontaneous and lackadaisical manner

An inclination toward avoidance

An optimistic manner

Among these three options, which one do you employ to confront the challenges of life?

Adverse Troubleshooting

Individuals who engage in negative problem-solving approaches perceive life's challenges as sources of threat and overwhelming circumstances. They possess minimal faith in their capacity to discover resolutions. They doubt their skills. They express internal thoughts such as "This task proves to be exceedingly challenging." I do not possess the capability to take any action in this situation. This issue is incapable of resolution. There seems to be a lack of a definitive response." Their negative perspective hinders their pursuit of potential remedies, thus diminishing the likelihood of achieving satisfactory outcomes. Negative problem solving is delineated by two of the aforementioned styles, namely an impetuous and heedless approach, as well as an evasive approach. Both options are undesirable, and should you opt for either one, it is essential that you modify your approach. As elucidated in the preceding chapter, it is often prudent to temporarily abstain from engaging with a troublesome circumstance or individual as a means to mitigate feelings of anger. Having the wisdom to discern which circumstances to evade and which to confront is a pivotal factor in navigating the adversities of life. We would like to emphasize that evading or eluding the situation is deemed appropriate solely within a limited timeframe. Engaging in such a practice as a long-term strategy for addressing significant life matters is not advisable.

As time progresses, the propensity to evade can exacerbate certain issues, precipitating heightened levels of vexation, apprehension, and indignation. The accounts of Mark and Marjorie exemplify the collective consequences of Mark's impulsive approach and Marjorie's avoidant approach to confronting the various trials of life.

Mark, a carpenter aged thirty-two, has been consistently troubled by intense anger responses throughout his adult years. One particular matter of relevance pertained to his vehemence exhibited during his operation of a vehicle. He would engage in aggressive driving behavior such as accelerating, closely following other vehicles, and vocalizing offensive language towards those who merged abruptly or drove at a slow pace. He acted on impulse, without giving due consideration to the potential consequences.

In a notable occurrence, Mark pursued a vehicle that had abruptly changed lanes in front of him, eventually employing force to divert it from the road. Once both vehicles had halted on the side of the road, Mark hastily disembarked to reprimand the other driver. However, as Mark neared the vicinity of the adjacent vehicle, the driver of the latter menacingly brandished a firearm in his direction. This incident greatly impacted Mark, however, it did not result in a modification of his conduct. Indeed, subsequently, he was apprehended on multiple occasions for engaging in reckless driving and, ultimately, suffered the revocation of his driver's license. Following each of his apprehensions, Mark professed remorse for his actions, yet they persisted to such an extent that he even engaged in unauthorized driving for a period of several months. While traversing the streets, amidst fervent circumstances, he seldom took into account viable courses of action to handle discourteous fellow drivers. Mark was left with no alternative but to engage in confrontation. Mark encountered comparable challenges in his professional environment. Despite possessing a commendable work ethic, he proved incapable of effectively managing conflicts. For instance, when faced with minor critique from his supervisor or a colleague, Mark would spontaneously embark on an extensive, enraged discourse, lambast the critic, and on occasion, indulge in physical altercations. Furthermore, in the event of customer dissatisfaction, Mark displayed a disposition to disregard any criticism and promptly associated the customer with characteristics such as being overly meticulous, entitled, and unreasonably demanding. Furthermore, there were instances where he displayed a deliberate lack of concern resulting in the damage of various properties.

Mark's tendency to exhibit impulsive and anger-driven behaviors manifested on an almost daily basis. Overtime, these displays of anger diminished his interpersonal connections, hindered his professional trajectory, and gave rise to a multitude of supplementary challenges that he had to contend with.

Marjorie, an articulate and sociable individual in her late thirties, served as a counselor within a nonprofit organization. Having recently undergone a divorce, she was the mother of two children, ages six and eight. Additionally, she encountered a significant amount of financial strain, resulting in a continual conflict with her former spouse regarding his inconsistent compliance with the court-ordered child support payments. Marjorie was encountering difficulties in her professional environment as well. She had difficulty establishing a positive rapport with her immediate superior and had consistently been denied promotions that she believed she merited.

At first glance, it seemed that Marjorie possessed the requisite personal attributes to manage the demands of life. However, she seldom confronted her issues head-on. She conscientiously steered clear of encountering individuals with whom she anticipated a potential clash and optimistically entrusted matters to resolve on their own. As an instance, rather than retaining the services of legal counsel to ensure her husband's adherence to the child support agreement, she postponed engaging with an attorney and relied on the expectation that her former spouse would voluntarily fulfill his obligations. Instead of actively seeking alternative employment, she adopted a patient demeanor, anticipating the departure of her supervisor. Marjorie's difficulties worsened as a result of her lack of action. As her challenges accumulated and intensified, she experienced a mounting sense of being overwhelmed.

As time progressed, her life descended into disarray. However, when Marjorie was questioned about her intended course of action regarding the turmoil she faced, she simply stated, "Numerous individuals find themselves in circumstances akin to my own." I am skeptical about the existence of a genuine solution."

Her everyday existence was predominantly consumed by emotions of anger, bitterness, and sadness. The impacts of Mark's and Marjorie's social problem-solving patterns on their lives are readily apparent. In the event that you possess a negative approach to social problem solving, akin to that of Mark and Marjorie, there exists a glimmer of optimism. Through determined exertion, it is plausible to alter your decision-making process and reformulate your reactions towards the inescapable vexations that life presents.

The Developmental Phases

When contemplating the concept of development, progress inevitably comes to mind. Consequently, we can interpret growth as the process by which a child gradually attains self-sufficiency to the extent that they cease to rely on their parents.

There is much complexity that needs to be analyzed and understood within this context.

In the first place, the conception of development revolves around the notion of "autonomy." Consequently, the progress of children primarily hinges on their capacity to progressively diminish their dependence on their parents. Certain children may require more time compared to their peers. Certain individuals fail to achieve complete autonomy and continue to depend on their parents well into their adult years. These individuals, well into their forties, rely on their parents for financial support due to an inability to secure employment or manage their own affairs.

I am positive that you have encountered similar circumstances previously.

This notion is not intended to serve as an accusation. Although these instances are relatively infrequent, they serve to illustrate the importance of cultivating autonomy during youth in order to facilitate a smooth transition into adulthood. Kindly bear in mind that the primary aim of children's development is to acquire the skills necessary to navigate their surroundings. Put simply, it is essential for them to obtain the necessary skills and resources to effectively maneuver through the challenges they encounter in practical situations.

Consider this:

Children engage in negotiation on a regular basis. For example, when children engage in play, they are required to engage in negotiations pertaining to various matters, including the choice of games, the equitable division of playtime, and the adherence to rules within the game. It is imperative for children to cultivate proficient negotiating abilities. Alternatively, children might encounter challenges in interacting with their peers, potentially resulting in feelings of social isolation and subsequent emotional repercussions.

When contemplating the progression of your offspring, it is of utmost importance to direct attention towards the essential elements indispensable for their triumph in society. Frequently, our thinking revolves around a customary array of instruments, such as the acquisition of literacy skills. However, there exist certain tools that are imperative for children to acquire at distinct stages of their growth and development. Their ability to transition from one stage to the next is enhanced when they do so.

Consider it from this perspective: when a child attains expertise in a particular stage, they will encounter greater convenience in progressing to the subsequent stage. This process exhibits a compounding effect. As a result, your child effectively integrates and builds upon acquired skills, thereby exhibiting a cumulative influence on their holistic growth.

Chronic anger

This pervasive discontent frequently extends to others and is often channeled inward, resulting in self-directed anger. Frequent irritation tends to be a common characteristic, and the persistent nature of it can eventually have detrimental consequences on your overall welfare.

To effectively manage this form of anger, it is recommended to allocate a period for introspection regarding potential anger-inducing factors. Upon determining the trigger, you will be better equipped to address your internal conflict by simply allowing yourself to undergo a process of forgiveness for any past transgressions. The process of forgiveness holds immense importance as it aids in effectively addressing the anguish and distress that you may have been persevering through.

Critical anger

This is a surge of moral indignation frequently aimed at a perceived inequity. Whilst this particular form of anger assumes an attitude of justified moral superiority, it can prompt you to alienate your friends by simply dismissing their viewpoints.

One optimal approach for addressing this particular manifestation of anger involves dedicating time to thoroughly examine a variety of scenarios, which, despite appearing straightforward at first glance, possess intricate underlying intricacies. Put simply, the viewpoint of others can be immensely beneficial in offering valuable insights into potential resolutions to the prevailing issue.

Self-abusive anger

This phenomenon is alternatively referred to as anger stemming from a sense of shame. This implies that in instances where one has experienced heightened desperation and humiliation, there is a tendency to internalize these emotions and manifest a burning anger through negative internal discourse and self-inflicted harm. Additional individuals may seek solace in unhealthy eating habits and the misuse of substances, resulting in diminished self-worth and a sense of disconnection from their peers.

In order to address this anger, it is imperative to employ cognitive reformulation techniques to systematically confront and overcome the self-destructive thoughts that are currently being encountered.

Mindfulness meditation can also prove to be quite efficacious in addressing impulsive tendencies.

Verbal anger

This form of anger is classified as psychological abuse, which intends to inflict harm upon individuals believed to be responsible for initiating acts of violence. It may manifest through the use of intimidating tactics, mocking and belittling remarks, derogatory statements, assigning fault, and vocal outbursts, among various forms of verbal indications. Feelings of shame are also present in conjunction with this, and are often followed by subsequent feelings of regret.

Regarding this anger, it is of utmost importance that you carefully consider the consequences your words may have on your lips before expressing them. Indeed, it is undoubtedly alluring to surrender to the impulse of letting go, yet it is imperative to bear in mind that the crux of managing anger lies in postponing the inclination to retaliate. Through consistent practice, it will become evident to you that the inclination towards engaging in verbal abuse can be minimized, and in its place, you can proficiently adopt assertive forms of communication.

Develop a tool for monitoring triggers.

Assisting your child in examining situations that frequently trigger their emotional reactions enables them to cultivate heightened self-awareness and eventually enhance their ability to cope with challenging circumstances by employing problem-solving skills and proactive measures.

Please obtain a sheet of paper and create a series of checkboxes vertically aligned on the left-hand margin of the page. If your child is of a more tender age, it will be necessary for you to identify and address potential catalysts for anger. An elder child could be requested to aid in the compilation of a list.

Anger scale

This activity establishes meaningful connections between multiple essential elements encompassing anger management for children. It underscores the concept that anger manifests in different intensities and degrees. In order to establish an anger scale with your child, you may utilize a straightforward box graph representation (illustrated below) or a basic depiction of an 'anger thermometer.' Both visual aids facilitate the child's recognition of anger triggers, as well as the observable transformation of their facial expressions and features as a consequence of anger. If you are employing the thermometer analogy, place a numerical value of ten at the upper end and a numerical value of one at the lower end, thereby encouraging your child to contemplate instances and entities that evoke their anger, and subsequently determine the appropriate placement on the spectrum. It may come as a surprise as to where certain things eventually find themselves!

Strategies for Mitigating Undesirable Behavior

Be consistent.

The uniformity of laws plays a vital role in instructing children on how to make sound judgments. If a child consistently faces consequences for throwing a toy, such as temporarily losing access to it, they will acquire the understanding that throwing toys is an undesirable behavior. Nevertheless, due to the ever-evolving nature of legislation, young children encounter challenges when attempting to make astute judgements. If an outburst fails to persuade your child to prolong their stay at the park on one occasion, but results in them taking an additional four trips down the slide the following day, they may experience uncertainty in choosing an approach, thinking, "Well, displaying agitation proved effective previously, so perhaps I should attempt that once more."

Stop bargaining.

This is hard. It is our aspiration for our children to experience a sense of being listened to. We strive to be perceived as individuals who possess open-mindedness and actively engage in attentive listening. We aim to demonstrate flexibility. Nevertheless, engaging in negotiations concerning familial regulations can be a perilous endeavor. A child who possesses the skills to engage in negotiation in order to secure extra cookies or a postponement of bedtime will swiftly recognize the potency of this strategy in acquiring these "perquisites." Consequently, you will soon encounter a situation where negotiation becomes the norm for every aspect of interaction. Establishing and enforcing uniform regulations concerning activities such as hand-holding in parking lots, adherence to car seat usage, and thorough teeth brushing contributes to fostering a sense of safety and stability for children. They come to the realization that their cosmos exhibits systematicity, rationality, and coherence.

Allow them to problem-solve.

Encourage independent problem-solving in your child by refraining from intervening prematurely. Encourage your child to independently find a resolution, be it locating the appropriate spot for the puzzle piece they hold or engaging in a negotiation with a friend regarding the first turn on the swing. (Should individuals approach you seeking assistance in addressing the matter, you can facilitate their progress by offering suggestions: The intricate nature of building blocks can be quite daunting! Perhaps consider augmenting the lower portion of the structure with additional blocks, so as to prevent its collapse?) You may be pleasantly surprised by their remarkable ability to navigate conflicts and effectively manage the challenges that come their way.

Offer generous commendation to your child when they exhibit self-discipline.

Children possess a strong desire to elicit approval. By responding in a favorable manner to their actions, you bolster and enhance their abilities and concurrently augment their level of confidence. Instead of resorting to physical violence, you expressed your frustration by stomping your feet. Remarkable job! Children who possess a positive self-perception are inclined towards demonstrating exemplary behavior. It is imperative to assist children in gaining firsthand exposure to and understanding of the inherent advantages of exhibiting proper behavior.

What It Symbolises And Common Qualities

Authoritative parenting is distinguished by the imposition of substantial expectations upon one's child, coupled with a significant degree of empathic comprehension. Therefore, although authoritative parents demonstrate warmth and cultivate their child's independence, they consistently establish limits and administer appropriate discipline when required.

Typically, parents of this nature do not make demands for respect; rather, they actively work towards earning it. They cultivate their children's upbringing by nurturing them with affection as well as fostering a sense of discipline, effectively striking a harmonious equilibrium in their parental approach. While fostering open communication, explicit boundaries are established to ensure that they are not violated. Authoritative parents employ explanations and mutual reasoning instead of resorting to threats, raised voices, or punishments when they wish to convey their point. An authoritative parent positions themselves in a manner that embodies the balance between firmness and fairness.

▷ Illustrations of parenting characterized by a firm yet nurturing approach

Several practical examples showcasing the implementation of authoritative parenting encompass:

In the event that a child engages in the act of toy throwing, rather than reacting with raised voices and exclamation, an authoritative parent will take the opportunity to explicate the potential repercussions of such behavior, including the risk of harm to others. Subsequently, the parent presents the repercussions of engaging in such behavior once more. For example, if the child persists in throwing the toy after the parent has provided an explanation regarding the repercussions, the parent may choose to confiscate the toy and remark to the child, "it appears that you are not yet prepared to engage responsibly with this toy." I will store it away and provide you with another opportunity to try in the future.

Envision a young child displaying anger. During the initial phases of a child's development, comprehending emotions can prove to be a challenge as they are unfamiliar to toddlers. Authoritative parents have recognized and acknowledged the emotions of their child in this regard. They acknowledge their child's emotional state by expressing, 'It appears that you are experiencing distress because you are unwilling to depart from the park at this moment.' "However, it is now the appropriate time to depart and you have two options: you may either proceed to the vehicle on foot or engage in a playful manner reminiscent of a hopping bunny." This approach conveys to the child that their emotions are acknowledged and honored, while redirecting their attention away from distress by granting them the autonomy to decide between walking or bunny-like movements towards the car.

4. Hindered goals

Obstructed objectives often serve as a common catalyst for frustration within the professional realm. Attaining objectives is commonly associated with achieving professional success. Performance evaluations, salary enhancements, career advancements, esteem, and acknowledgement typically stem from goal-oriented endeavors and significantly influence an individual's professional trajectory. When the advancement towards objectives is impeded, it may provoke resentment due to the ramifications it could potentially have on professional trajectories.

Objectives are prone to impediment when the goals of one individual or collective vary from those of another individual or collective. In larger organizations, this is typically the prevailing standard as opposed to being an anomaly.

For example, during the pursuit of long-term objectives set by the organization, it is possible that the objectives of various departments and individuals within the organization may diverge.

Nevertheless, short-term objectives are exceedingly prone to diverge, thereby presenting a greater potential for hindrances and subsequent provocation of anger.

In the event that a software developer is in the process of developing a novel program, it has come to their attention that a competitor is strategizing to unveil a software solution that bears resemblance to theirs. The management is experiencing the imperative need to outperform this competitor in terms of market entry, as failure to do so could result in the forfeiture of significant market share. Consequently, due to the aforementioned circumstances, the management exerts pressure on the software development team to expedite project completion.

This obstructs the achievement of objectives and engenders frustration among all parties involved. The programmers are dissatisfied with their team leader as they are unable to produce work of high quality while maintaining a sustainable rate of progress. The team leader is displeased with management due to the inefficiency of her programmers. As the programmers experience exhaustion, there has been an increase in the occurrence of quality issues and mistakes. This elicits discontent from the management towards the team leader, as his objectives of attaining both quality and efficiency are not being met.

Question

Which statements exemplify instances of workplace frustration resulting from impeded objectives?

Options:

Ted is experiencing frustration as he consistently communicates about the systemic constraints that lead to disruptions, yet no measures are taken to enhance the said system.

Emily is currently experiencing frustration as numerous employees have been disregarding her requests for employee contact information verification.

Cosmo experiences displeasure when his superior declines his appeal for essential resources required to successfully conclude a project within the designated timeframe.

Kim is deeply resentful of the fact that George earns a higher income than her, despite the absence of any significant disparity in their intelligence or level of education.

Answer

Alternative 1: This option is not correct. Alternative 2: Regrettably, this option is incorrect. Alternative 3: It is with great certainty that I state this option to be incorrect. The source of Ted's anger stems from his discontentment with the system. Despite him reporting a problem with productivity, no effective measures are ever taken to address the issue.

Alternative two: This choice is accurate. Emily is filled with frustration towards her coworkers due to the obstruction they are causing in her quest to validate employee contact information.

Option 3: This option is accurate. Cosmo's fury stems from the obstruction of his objectives. Without the resources that his boss declined to authorize, he will not be able to accomplish his objective of finishing his project within the designated timeframe.

Choice 4: This selection is not accurate. Kim's anger stems from her perception of being subjected to unfair treatment. She holds the belief that George is receiving a greater share than she is, despite making a lesser contribution.

5. Dissimilar values

An additional factor contributing to workplace anger is the presence of divergent values. Contrary to personal values that often vary, professional values are commonly held and greatly valued in work settings. When these values are not accorded due respect or consideration, it has the potential to elicit feelings of anger in individuals.

Reflect

What are some prevalent shared values among employees in a workplace, in your opinion?

Kindly articulate your reflections within the designated area. After completion, please proceed to click on the 'Next Page' button to acquire further information regarding prevalent workplace values.

Please record your response by either writing it down or entering it into a text file using a word-processing application. You may also use a text editor like Notepad. Remember to save the file on your hard drive so that you can access it later.

The workplace values that are most frequently shared include proficiency, diligence, and honesty. When individuals converge on these ideals, it is probable that employees will effectively collaborate and foster a harmonious work environment. On the other hand, when individuals witness a lack of respect or infringement upon these principles, it can evoke feelings of anger.

Examine each value in order to understand its practical implications within the professional setting.

Needs

Emotional equilibrium remains elusive if our fundamental needs remain unfulfilled. Individuals who are experiencing emotional disturbances pertaining to anger possess unmet psychological needs that are not being adequately addressed. This is consistently the scenario as individuals do not deliberately opt to exhibit aggression and intense anger. Rather, it is driven by a psychological imperative.

A fundamental psychological necessity that the majority of individuals necessitate within this domain is affection. Love fosters a sense of stability within an individual, and individuals who experience love in their lives are endowed with a profound sense of security. In the absence of love, conversely, the inverse holds. An individual experiences a decline in mental stability and feelings of inadequacy, which give rise to psychological issues encompassing anger.

Insufficient affection may have arisen in one's childhood owing to the presence of parents who exhibited negligence and absence. Nevertheless, every relationship holds significance, whether it be a platonic friendship or a romantic union. In the absence of such relationships in one's life, or the collapse of relationships due to a lack of profound connection, one may develop a belief that they are incapable of being loved.

Additionally aggravating the matter, an individual who has consistently experienced a lack of affection tends to develop increased emotional dependence on others, seeking their validation and contentment. The emotions of being unlovable are exacerbated by feelings of inadequacy and reliance.

Below are several instances in which individuals may experience feelings of anger and fury due to the absence of love in their lives:

A woman frequently finds herself single due to the lack of success in her romantic relationships with men. As she advances in age, her acquaintances enter into matrimonial unions and establish households, leading her to believe that she may never encounter romantic love or experience the joys of domestic life.

A young man is unable to establish a connection with his peers. Despite his efforts to establish connections, he consistently fails to integrate within any social circle, frequently finding himself isolated and experiencing a pervasive sense of emotional neglect.

A young lady is distressed by a companion within her social circle who consistently undermines her fashion sense and demeanor, and the woman's acquaintances tolerate this behavior without reproach. Frequently, she harbors the perception that her acquaintances' affection towards her is insincere, despite their verbal assertions.

The woman consistently experiences agitation and dissatisfaction in regards to her occupation, while her husband perceives her discontent as a reflection of their marriage, sensing annoyance towards him and a lingering desire to have married another individual.

Strategies for Effectively Handling Provocations of Anger

After gaining an understanding of your triggers, presented here are several strategies that can be employed to effectively cope with them and regulate your anger.

Exercise restriction in engaging with individuals exhibiting toxic behavior.

If engaging in or being in the presence of someone elicits feelings of extreme anger, it is advisable to curtail your interactions with that individual until such time as you are able to exercise more effective emotional regulation. In order to maintain a healthy environment for yourself, it is advisable to distance yourself from any form of negativity or toxicity. If someone is introducing such elements into your life, it would be prudent to sever communication with them.

Commence the process by acknowledging the detrimental influences present in your life, including but not limited to an abusive romantic partner, a toxic acquaintance, a domineering sibling, or any other individual who causes distress or upheaval. If you are not residing in close proximity with an individual or maintaining frequent interactions with them, it would be advisable to refrain from answering their phone calls. If necessary, you may opt to block their contact details. If the individual persists in pestering you, it is important to assertively communicate your unwillingness to remain in contact with them.

In the case of individuals such as colleagues, a significant other, immediate family members, and other individuals whom it is impractical to completely avoid and with whom regular interaction is required, it is advisable to tune out any distressing remarks. In the event that any of their actions provoke your frustration, it is important to acknowledge that although you may offer them counsel, you cannot exert authority over them, thus it is prudent to relinquish control.

Practice Deep Breathing

Research has conclusively demonstrated that engaging in shallow and rapid respiration serves as a catalyst for the onset of stress and anger. Upon facing a difficult or perilous circumstance, an immediate physiological reaction manifests in the form of an accelerated heart rate, subsequently causing an elevation in one's respiration rate. Upon reception of this signal by the brain, there is an elevation in the secretion of the stress hormone. The same phenomenon occurs when one experiences anger, which explains why shallow breathing is often referred to as "angry breathing" in scientific discourse.

In order to effect a positive change, it is advisable to engage in deep breathing exercises whenever circumstances allow. Deep diaphragmatic breathing elicits a sense of tranquility, diminishes the concentration of stress-inducing hormones within the body, and enhances cognitive processing capabilities. When one engages in rational thinking, it is probable that their response to anger will be more measured, rather than impulsive, thus facilitating the reduction of their rage. Participate in the practice of prolonged breathing exercises for a minimum duration of 5 minutes on a daily basis.

Please adopt a comfortable seated position within a tranquil space, preferably a secluded section of a room, and proceed to engage in inhalation for a duration of 5 seconds. Gently and gradually release your breath, incrementing the count to reach 7 or 8. Exhale for a slightly extended duration compared to your typical breath, while maintaining a composed state. In a state of anger, respiration increases. The key to achieving a state of calmness resides in exhaling more deliberately. By engaging in the 5:7 breathing exercise for a duration of 5 minutes, an enhanced sense of tranquility will be experienced.

Participate in this activity on a daily basis regardless of whether you experience anger or not, with a particular emphasis on engaging in the practice when you are feeling angry. As you endeavor to cultivate this habit, it is recommended that you engage in the practice of deep breathing more frequently, allocating approximately 5 minutes for this exercise, ideally 3 to 5 times per day and prior to retiring for the night. In a span of one month, marked enhancements in your capacity to maintain composure and exercise mastery over your anger shall become apparent.

Efficiently oversee and strategize the organization and coordination of tasks.

If your frustration stems from a deficiency in organization, management, and planning, it would be beneficial to enhance your skill in these areas by implementing improved planning and management strategies. In order to avoid experiencing frustration each morning due to departing from home late for work as a result of staying up late, consider establishing an earlier bedtime routine to facilitate waking up punctually. If you react harshly to your children's untidiness in their room, it is advisable to establish clear boundaries for them. If the lack of organization and order in your household and daily routine are causing heightened frustration, it is advisable to promptly attend to cleaning tasks, establish a system of organization, engage in regular decluttering, and establish a weekly plan for tasks, keeping a readily accessible to-do list.

Persistent anger does not manifest suddenly; rather, it typically arises from prolonged periods of frustration that gradually accumulate and transform into a formidable force. Upon initiating the process of effectively overseeing and arranging your tasks and daily responsibilities, discernible decreases in your overall emotional state of anger will become apparent.

Chronic anger

If an individual experiences immediate expression of anger through behavior, chronic anger persists like an unresolved, persistent injury. More precisely, it pertains to a form of broad animosity towards individuals, situations, occurrences or even oneself that has the potential to endure over prolonged periods of time, spanning weeks, months, or even years. It commonly manifests through persistent irritation, which can significantly impact an individual's physical and psychological well-being.

One pragmatic approach to addressing this particular manifestation of anger is to conduct a sincere examination into the underlying factors that precipitate such intense feelings, delving beyond superficial observations. Although it may require a significant amount of time, delving into the underlying cause of your resentment will enable you to ultimately relinquish your anger. This frequently manifests as granting forgiveness for a previous transgression, leading to a profound emotional release.

Judgmental anger

This form of anger frequently assumes the guise of justified moral outrage, although it extends beyond rectifying a genuine wrongdoing and can be instigated by something trivial such as a perceived offense or an observed deficiency in another individual. Whilst this form of anger may initially lead one to believe that they hold the moral superiority, it is highly likely that they are, in fact, being equally disrespectful towards others by disregarding their personal viewpoints. Passing judgment on individuals whom one is unacquainted with or who have not transgressed against oneself is a prevalent manifestation of critical animosity.

Although it can be challenging to manage this form of anger in the present moment, the most effective strategy to mitigate its impact in the long run is to consistently and intentionally cultivate empathy towards others. Additionally, it is imperative to develop a routine of consistently engaging in this behavior, rather than sporadically engaging in it, as it is essential to fully dedicate oneself to the act whenever one senses an increase in judgmental anger. Depending on how set in your angry ways you are, this might be an extremely difficult exercise to get the hang of at first, but if you persevere it will get easier each time you manage to do so successfully.

Overwhelming anger

This form of anger is universally encountered occasionally, arising when individuals encounter challenging circumstances that surpass their ability to regulate or influence. Frequently, it engenders a combination of exasperation and despair. When confronted with the sudden realization of overwhelming responsibilities and the inability to alter one's course, or when unforeseen life events adversely affect one's well-being, it is quite common to experience such emotions. However, it is imperative to acknowledge that if this anger begins to manifest itself in response to relatively trivial occurrences, it has the potential to disrupt one's daily life. Afterwards, it becomes increasingly challenging for you to carry out essential activities in a regular manner.

The prevailing sense of despair associated with this form of rage can render it exceedingly challenging to cope with independently. Therefore, if you perceive an excessive intensity of anger such as this, it is crucial to seek assistance from a qualified professional.

www.ingramcontent.com/pod-product-compliance
Lightning Source LLC
Chambersburg PA
CBHW052138110526
44591CB00012B/1769